Around &

SIDMOUTH

Chips Barber
and
Sally Barber

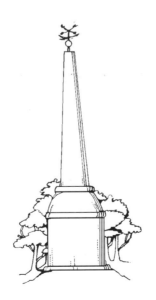

OBELISK PUBLICATIONS

PLATE ACKNOWLEDGEMENTS
All colour photographs by Chips Barber
Ann Dunford for pages 4 and 8, Mr Hendy for page 26, Jeff Bowden for page 11, Stuart
Hughes for page 19, Ronald A. Lumber for page 15, Rodney Tucker for page 22.

First published in 1993 by
Obelisk Publications, 2 Church Hill, Pinhoe, Exeter, Devon
Designed by Chips and Sally Barber
Typeset by Sally Barber
Printed in Great Britain by
Sprint Print Co Ltd, Okehampton Place, Exeter

Around & About Sidmouth

This is a book that I hope visitors might like to take home with them. I have tried to make it a bit 'different', by weaving together some of the more unusual trivia and stories associated with Sidmouth. Included for your edification are just some of the comings and goings, personalities and places 'around and about' the resort. If you imagine all of Sidmouth's history and geography being like one giant photographic album, then this little book is just a selection of some of the more interesting and unusual 'snap shots'. For good measure I have included some of the nearby places like Salcombe Regis, Sidbury, Sidford and Otterton, all of which look on Sidmouth as their main town.

My association with Sidmouth goes 'way back'. Apart from the numerous 'talks' given to local groups, I actually spent many days here, in my youth, doing traffic surveys – but I accept no blame for the one-way system that, at times, almost exhibits as many foibles and eccentricities as some members of the local population!

The town has had many distinguished visitors throughout the years and vied with Torquay for the distinction of having more 'Royals' per square mile than anywhere else in the world! However we start our look at the resort by remembering two aristocratic visitors with a difference…

Older Sidmothians may remember the wreckage lying on the beach up to about 1950. It was then, after littering the beach for sixteen years, that the final bits were hauled away, so ending a romantic story of not only a grand old lady, but a Duchess!

The *Duchess of Devonshire* (170 feet long and 221 tons) is shown here in all her glory, at Sidmouth, being a frequent visitor. Her male counterpart, the slightly larger *Duke of Devonshire* tended to operate farther west in the county. By clever planning, it was

possible to travel on both the *Duke* and the *Duchess* on the same day, covering most of the South and East Devon coastlines.

These paddle steamers were built by the London firm of R. & H. Green of Blackwall, specialists in clipper-ships. With their steel structures they were designed to land on steeply shelving shingle beaches (Sidmouth had one then). The *Duchess* made frequent similar landings at West Bay, Seaton and Budleigh Salterton for there were no jetties or piers for her to use like the ones at Teignmouth or Torquay. Her Captain, a gentleman called Carter, who lived at Pinhoe on the eastern outskirts of Exeter, was a master of the art of landing her at beaches like Sidmouth. However there were times when those who bought a ticket for a trip that should have brought them back to Sidmouth, found that a change in the wind, weather and wave conditions forced them to disembark, up the coast, at Exmouth!

But there were compensations for she ran to time and was dependable. A cruise from Lyme Regis, pausing at her regular ports of call, before reaching Teignmouth Pier, would last about three hours. The landings at Sidmouth were quite an experience as it was necessary for passengers disembarking to walk down a flexible gangplank, which had a fair amount of spring. Those inexperienced landlubbers with the wrong technique ran the risk of being catapulted several inches off the ground; occasionally they were even propelled into the briny!

However one bonus was the way in which the public were informed of arrival and departure times at Sidmouth; the Town Crier, Theo Mortimore, complete in all his splendid regalia, would bawl out the details.

As the storm clouds of war formed over Europe, the *Duke* and the *Duchess* embarked on one last round of voyages along the coast. One outing, which was well supported, was from Sidmouth, using both paddle steamers, to go to Torquay. The attraction was the spectacle of seeing Britain's challenger for The Americas Cup Race, a graceful yacht called *Shamrock*, go through her paces.

During the First World War the *Duchess* was sent to Bristol where she became a familiar sight lying beneath Brunel's great piece of Victorian design, the Clifton Suspension Bridge. Circumstances though didn't give her the chance to rest and relax as she was commissioned to operate a cross Bristol Channel service between Weston-super-Mare and the 'foreign' port of Cardiff.

The late 1920s were notoriously tough years and a large proportion of the population either didn't have the financial means or the inclination to indulge in short sea cruises on vessels like the *Duke* and the *Duchess of Devonshire*. In 1930 she was laid up at Exmouth and sat out the next few seasons, her yellow funnel a familiar landmark to all those who went about their daily work at the docks. However the *Duke* was sold and the *Duchess* was refitted, repainted and refurbished for one last fling on the high seas! Smartly attired in an appropriate 'Royal' blue, with a bright white but blue-ringed funnel, she set out to once more delight locals and trippers alike. It was all plain sailing until one fateful day in late August 1934. In order to land at Sidmouth she had to

4

manoeuvre her bow end to the shore. Alas the rope from her stern anchor snapped and she swung around. To the astonishment of her owner and captain, who looked on helplessly, she was washed broadsides onto Sidmouth Beach. The event made the front page of the national press, the *Daily Mirror* carrying a heart-rending picture in its 28 August edition. A few days later the paper stated that, "the *Duchess* has been left to her doom!"

There were times when Sidmouth had its own lifeboat – the *Rimington*, a vessel that enjoyed a few close shaves! Being a boat you would have thought, quite reasonably, that when she was delivered to the resort, she would have arrived by sea. Not so. She arrived at Honiton, some eight miles away, by train; Sidmouth was not connected by the railway then. Transporting her over the top of the steep Gittisham Hill was a slow and tedious affair, but worthwhile as cheering crowds lined the streets of Sidbury, and then Sidford, as she passed down the valley and into Sidmouth.

The eight horses who had the unenviable task of pulling her all the way, were given a meal guaranteed to satisfy any horse's appetite!

A few days later a grand ceremony was organized to unveil the boat. Although there were marching bands, bunting and a number of dignitaries in attendance, there were still a few hiccoughs. The triumphal arches were not tall enough for the lifeboat to pass through and several were accidentally demolished in the process!

One of the *Rimington*'s few scrapes with stormy seas occurred in 1883 when Prince Alfred, The Duke of Edinburgh, had to be rescued. He was aboard the pinnace HMS *Lively*, which lived up to her name and came close to capsizing a short way off Sidmouth. Although the Duke was grateful to be rescued, he was in a sodden state and had to rely on the good folk of Sidmouth to bale him out (literally). A local lady kindly lent the royal entourage her carriage so they could get to Exmouth. On arriving there the Duke's problems continued as his carriage ran into an omnibus.

Another incident occurred farther out to sea in 1907 when the Brixham fishing ketch, the *Skylark* spotted what they thought was a hay-rick floating in the sea. However a closer inspection of the strange find showed it to be an unoccupied army observation balloon. The attempts to secure and inspect it verged on the comical, with the balloon tantalizingly staying always that little bit ahead of the fishing boat. But Brixham craft are used to catching things. A bold effort ended with the basket, which was normally suspended beneath the balloon, being attached to the fishing boat long enough to see that all it contained was a riding crop! The boat let it go and continued to fish for another three days before returning to Brixham. The discovery was reported to the army, who sent two men from the Royal Engineers to investigate. It was revealed that the balloon had been manned by two officers who had set out from Aldershot. It is probable that Sidmouth was the last place they saw before ditching into the sea – never to be seen again.

In March 1939, an hotelier, looking out of a sea-facing window at the Bedford Hotel, observed lights in the night sky circling around the bay. They gradually got lower until they suddenly stopped and were replaced by distress signals. He immediately rang Sidmouth's police station, who alerted the relevant rescue services. Toby Smith, an elderly local fisherman, quickly recruited his friends, Messrs Rickwood, Dagworthy and Parrett. It was a windy, dark night with a heavy sea. After a great deal of effort they reached an RAF plane floating on the surface after having executed a skilful crash landing. The crew of four were rescued but the small boat, with everyone safely aboard, could not get back to Sidmouth beach so headed up the coast and beached near Salcombe Regis. Exhausted, the fishermen and the airmen struggled back to Sidmouth along the energy-sapping shingle beach. Having reported back to the police station, they were taken to the Bedford Hotel for the night.

Meanwhile, the Exmouth Lifeboat had been launched and obviously communications in 1939 were not so good in those days as they had no idea that a rescue had been made. In stormy conditions they searched about off Sidmouth until, after hours of being tossed

6

around on heavy seas, they returned to Exmouth. They had set out at 8.30 p.m. and got home at 3.45 a.m. some seven long hours later. According to reports, nobody moaned – they all accepted it as a necessary act.

Had Sidmouth had its own harbour, the fishermen may have got back to shore more quickly. There had been grand plans, a century earlier, to create one and it's possible that had they done so the beach may have suffered less shingle removal than it has done, particularly in recent years.

In 1835 a new sea wall was constructed and many businessmen thought that a harbour would add to the trade and prosperity of the town. A meeting was convened, which some eighty influential men attended. By July 1836 'An Act for making and maintaining a Harbour' had been given Royal Assent by William IV.

The plan was to create a pair of L-shaped piers that would enclose an area of about ten acres embracing Chit Rocks. To import the vast amount of shingle needed, a wooden railway was constructed between the eastern end of the sea front, near Alma Bridge, to Hook Ebb. But this was no easy task as they had to tunnel into the red sandstone Salcombe Hill Cliff for a third of a mile before emerging at the foot of the cliffs. From here the rails were laid at the top of the beach past Salcombe Mouth. The nature of the task meant the original estimate of almost twelve thousand pounds was a grave miscalculation and that a completed project would be double the original amount. A local blacksmith built a locomotive, of sorts, but this proved hopelessly inadequate and a new one was sent for from Exmouth. However this was done without a great deal of forethought and, after a chaotic overland journey, it was found that the engine was too big for the tunnel; its only use was to give people rides on a railway set up along the Esplanade.

The venture got as far as naming the two piers. The west pier was named in honour of Grand Duchess Helene of Russia whilst the east pier was named in honour of Princess Victoria. The two foundation stones were officially unveiled on 24 May 1837, Victoria's birthday. What a day that must have been! There were speeches, processions, hymn singing, banquets and a three hour firework display. The workmen were given a substantial meal at the Marine Hotel, consisting of vast amounts of roast beef, plum pudding and an endless supply of Sir John Barleycorn, presumably the Victorian equivalent of Carling Black Label! However that winter saw a cessation of the work that never recommenced. The company, the machinery and the harbour all faded away into the sea-mists of time. Was it the threat of the coming of the railways to other more accessible ports, or was it a case of too much plum pudding? We shall never know.

The Grand Duchess Princess Helene stayed at 8 Fortfield Terrace in the summer of 1831. With her came various Counts and Countesses, and a staff of about a hundred – a full supporting act! She landed at Plymouth and made it (a long haul in those days) to Sidmouth without once stopping to change horses! Most of the spare rooms around the town were taken over to accommodate her retinue, which included her band. The band gave concerts around the town, which bearing in mind the nature of the International Folk Festival, staged every summer, may well have been setting a precedent all those years ago. Her stay of exactly two months ended on 24 August when the complete entourage left for Windsor Castle (some reports say Cheltenham) to stay with King William IV.

In stark contrast to all the rich and titled visitors, the local fishermen lived a tough, meagre existence. Amongst their ranks was one Stephen Reynolds who fought, tooth and nail, for better conditions and a better lifestyle for them. His master stroke at highlighting their plight is a novel that he wrote in 1909, called *Poor Man's House*. The response to it in the town was mixed and some accused him of overdramatising the lot of the fishermen, but farther afield it was regarded as a work of genius. The great thinkers and academics of the day heralded it as a masterpiece.

Stephen Reynolds was involved in a rescue on Friday, 21 October 1916 when *Grendon Hall* went aground on cliffs near the mouth of the Sid. The vessel had been on her way from France to the port of Barry in South Wales when a terrific storm erupted. Mother Nature turned up the special effects to create cracking thunder, which reverberated around the hills, great forks of lighting, which lit up the heavens, and a whooshing force twelve wind that swept the ship to shore. Peering from his window at his home, Ernest Bonner saw distress signals and the rescue was underway. Despite the atrocious conditions, all 27 men were safely taken off the stricken vessel. Their gratitude was immense and some time later a silver walking stick and letter of thanks were presented to Mr Bonner and his brave associates.

The fishermen lived in a close knit society and, although there was rivalry between them, great friendships were formed. A characteristic of such communities was the common use of nicknames, some of which defy logic. On the beach in the past, along with the boats hauled up on the shingle bank, tending their nets could be found: Neebie Woolley, Gully Bartlett (Henry Isaac Carslake Bartlett, who operated the Ladies' Bathing Machines!), Scrummer Smith, Tink and Tuzzy Harris, Gibberick Bastin and good old Dappy Pinn. Each family had their own pitch on the beach, where they kept their boats and dried their nets, which were close to their respective 'Poor Men's Houses.' With families like the Wares, Hooks, Farrants, Bagwells and so on, fathers passed on their skills to their sons. And so it went on until the living became even tougher and traditions went out the window.

There are some people who, if they are going to go down, make sure they go down fighting. Such an indomitable spirit was shown as a severe storm built up in Lyme Bay in 1824. Those that could retreated to the safety of friends' houses but Dame Partington decided to remain in her house by the sea and give as good as she got. In time the story of her stoic action spread across the globe. Seven years later, in 1831, The Rev. Sidney Smith made a speech, at Taunton, which was directed at the like-minded stubborness of the House of Lords, who had refused to kow-tow to mass demands for public reform. He cited the example of gallant, but stubborn, Mrs Partington who had tried to overcome overwhelming odds. "In the winter of 1824 there set in a great flood upon that town. The tide rose to an incredible height, the waves rushed in upon the houses and everything was threatened with destruction! In the midst of this sublime and terrible storm, Dame Partington, who lived upon the beach, was seen at the door of her house with mop and

Sidmouth, 1924

pattens, trundling her mop, squeezing out the sea water and vigorously pushing away the Atlantic Ocean. The Atlantic was roused, Mrs Partington's spirit was up; but I need not tell you that the contest was unequal. The Atlantic Ocean beat Mrs Partington. She was excellent with a slop or a puddle, but should not have meddled with a tempest!" The speech won acclaim and Benjamin Penhallow Shillaber of the

8

Here we have the Connaught Gardens, famed far and wide for their floral displays. They are sheltered from sea breezes and prevailing winds and are a favourite spot for visitors and locals alike.

Jacob's Ladder

Boston Post was so impressed with Mrs Partington that he put together a book called *The Life and Sayings of Mrs Partington* – and it immediately sold thousands of copies in America!

In early September 1992 another storm took place in Lyme Bay and for the umpteenth time the residents on the sea front got ready to play 'King Canute', but at least they had the use of sand bags! Although it's easy to make light of their plight, when a combination of onshore winds and Spring tides occur, living on the sea front is a terrifying experience. A local video shop owner realized that there might be some spectacular footage of film to capture so, armed with a camera, he moved about the resort filming the scenes from safe vantage points. Market Square was awash with water and some waves were higher than sea front hotels! Most of the townsfolk slept on, blissfully unaware, whilst the storm reached its peak before breakfast time. However as copies of the video were put on sale, everyone had the opportunity to see just how close Sidmouth came to a major disaster yet again!

Another film enthusiast went one step further in May 1940. Jim Hellier was the son of the landlord and landlady of the Horse and Groom (no longer a pub). He knew that the skittle alley at the back of the pub had seen better times and persuaded his parents to let him turn it into a cinema. 'The Skittle Alley Cinema' had fifty seats, appropriate decorations and lights that changed colours to add atmosphere. Jim had a passion and a talent for making films about the local area and it was these that entertained Sidmothians. Of the forty that he made, the gala performance was called 'Storm over Sidmouth' and, like his present day counterparts, graphically illustrated the plight of the town when certain conditions of wind and tide prevail. Another popular film with his patrons was the first he ever made – a journey from the source of the River Sid right down to its mouth at the end of the sea front. However, this imaginative little venture came to an abrupt end when Jim received his 'call-up' papers and was obliged to go and do some shooting of a less peaceful variety.

The resort has been the playground of royalty but it has also been the originator of its own kings! There used to be an isolated rockpile, a short distance offshore, called Chit Rock. For some unknown, possibly religious, reason the fishermen of Sidmouth held this rock in great esteem and each year featured it in a ceremony where a local fisherman would be crowned 'King of Chit'. Alas this was but a mere sandstone stack and a series of storms culminated with the destruction of the rock in the famous storm of 1824 and with it its throne-like seat. The last king was a fisherman called Bolt who lived in a humble abode on the beach. Outside on a pocket-handkerchief sized piece of grass he kept a cow and a pig.

Then of course there was the gentleman whose love of the sea extended to the construction of artefacts with a maritime connection. He went to meticulous lengths when designing and building a capstan inside his cottage. The only thing he failed to do was to measure the width of the doorway, which turned out to be too narrow to get the capstan out!

Black's *Guide to Dorset, Devon and Cornwall* in 1871 has this to say of Sidmouth: *"Imagine a narrow valley gently sloping to the sea between two hills, which stretch their arms around it to fend the blasts of winter. Imagine a bold open beach, protected from the billows by a four fold terrace of pebbles, and at the head of this natural rampart place a long broad walk, 1700 feet, affording an almost unequalled promenade. Build on the slope a neat clean town in the shape of a Y, the stem pointing inland toward the green heights of Harpford, Beacon, and Pennhill. Range a row of 'handsome lodging*

10

houses', hotels, and libraries along the beach – and you have before you Sidmouth!" A lot of people choose or select 'select' Sidmouth because it has a reputation for being, generally, a quiet resort. This statement is enhanced by some comments featured in an official guide book from about 1970. "Holidaymakers seeking the peace and quiet associated with Sidmouth will be interested to know that a bye-law passed by the Devon County Council makes it an offence for anyone to operate a wireless set in any street or public place, including parks, pleasure grounds, and beaches, so as to cause or suffer to be made any noise which is so loud, continuous or repeated as to give reasonable cause for annoyance to other persons."

Stephen Fry is a familiar face on our television screens, from comedy series to clever commercials and, as they say, 'his face is his fortune!' He penned an article for the Daily Telegraph in September 1990 about a forthcoming series of 'Jeeves and Wooster,' which kicked off with an episode filmed at Sidmouth. His comments about the resort reflected an astute appreciation of what the place is all about, whether it is 1933 or 1993: "Sidmouth caters for the more mature citizen. Bridge, not bingo; thin lemon-coloured cardigans rather than T-shirts; a putting green instead of crazy golf; stay-pressed leisure slacks before Levi 501s."

There were shades of 'Fawlty Towers' in his informed comments about those visitors who died at their holiday hotel: "There is an average of four deaths a week in the hotels of Sidmouth, I was told yesterday. It is the usual practice among the hoteliers to remove bodies from their hotel rooms at two o'clock in the morning, so as not to unsettle other guests. If you are going to hop the twig in Sidmouth, hop it late in the day, or you'll have a long cold wait for your coffin."

There is plenty of evidence 'around and about Sidmouth' that a great number of people are smitten with its beauty and wonderful setting. All sorts of dedications can be found, in particular on benches funded in the memory of some dear departed loved one. Perhaps none more deserving of recognition for the affection in which she was held in this part of Devon is Miss Anne Farewell Jones. Her generosity enabled the National Trust to purchase much of the land on the cliffs near Peak Hill, on the western edge of Sidmouth. Fifty oak trees were planted in her honour in November 1988 and a seat is dedicated to her memory on a high spot gazing down on her beloved Sidmouth.

Sidmouth's period architecture has not gone unnoticed by film-makers and when anything 'English' Victorian/Edwardian needs some location filming, its name is high

on the list of options. In my book *Made in Devon*, which deals with an amazing variety of films and television programmes shot in the county, Sidmouth features prominently. So if you want to discover details of a *Summer Story*, when Sidmouth played the part of Torquay, or hear about how Miss Marple solved some murders in a neat burst of an episode lasting about 50 minutes, then get the book!

However, these details of *Jeeves and Wooster* are not included in *Made in Devon* – because the book was published first! Filming took place in September 1990 and it was as if the town had gone back in time. Any unsuspecting visitor would probably have thought that the resort was really old fashioned as the Silver Band sat in a bandstand playing 'Maid of the Mountains', whilst children, neatly attired in those once fashionable sailor suits, ran around with shrimping nets. Authentic 1930s' bicycles and motor cars gave Sidmouth that credibility as little work needed to be done to mask the tell-tale signs of this decade. Sidmouth, with its fine buildings, was the perfect backdrop for this and many other period pieces.

There was a furore about the 1989 Sidmouth Guide Book. Some traders felt that the publication made Sidmouth look like Blackpool. There were comments like, "It's reminiscent of the psychedelic 1960s." Such constructive comments have resulted in successive guide books being a little more in keeping with Sidmouth's image!

There is nothing like tempting providence so, when the Duke of Kent proclaimed in early January 1820 that he felt so well he'd "outlive them all!" it's not surprising to note that by the end of that same month he had been packaged up in an enormous seven foot long coffin and trundled back to London! His invitingly fatalistic words were written to one of his brothers whilst he stayed in the resort, partly to recover his health and partly to hide away from his apparent lack of disposable wealth. Sidmouth was regarded as an ideal out-of-the-way spot to get away from the attentions of creditors and many Victorian 'visitors' were in a similar financial state. Here they felt safe and it was unlikely anyone would locate them. The Duke of Kent redirected all his mail through Salisbury!

The Duke and Duchess had arrived at Sidmouth on Christmas Eve 1819 having spent time in Germany shortly before. General Baynes had generously allowed them the use of Woolbrook Cottage (now The Royal Glen Hotel) and the surroundings revived the Duke's spirits. With them was the young Princess Victoria, just a babe in arms! The Duke was very proud of his new daughter and was happy to parade her to people whilst walking along the promenade. History could have taken a very different course had a young lad out 'potting' sparrows missed by an even greater margin than he did. His

pellet shot was misdirected through an open window of the room where the future queen lay quietly sleeping, and grazed her sleeve!

Meanwhile the Duke went out for walks whenever he could. Unfortunately for him, a sudden cold snap produced a snow storm and what began as a minor cold, the result of a seasonal soaking, soon developed into pneumonia, which greatly affected his lungs. His own 'very bold physician' was

12

immediately summoned and a variety of treatments were applied. Although the precise practical consequences may not be readily appreciated, the following were used – 'blisters', 'bleedings', 'cuppings' and 'leeches'. However none worked and two large coffins were quickly brought to accommodate the dead Duke, one for his body and one for his heart! They say it's an ill wind that blows nobody any good. The limelight was firmly focussed on Sidmouth and the visitor numbers were given a healthy boost after this black event.

The following year His Honour Sir Edward Bray returned to work at the Bloomsbury County Court having fully recovered from a severe bout of sciatica. His pronouncement was: "I strongly recommend every sciatica sufferer to go to Sidmouth, for they are sure of a cure!" He was full of praise for the climate and the Baths.

New and more luxurious baths were opened in 1894. Indeed had there been Trading Standards in those days they would have had a field day checking out some of the outrageous claims of cures that the various treatments could effect. An advert which appeared in print a short time before the new baths opened stated: "*Sidmouth Brine Baths, The Esplanade, for Ladies and Gentlemen, are now in the course of erection and are intended to open in the Spring of 1895. They will comprise Hot and Cold Immersion Baths, with Fresh or Sea Water and a good Swimming or Plunge Bath, together with Needle Baths, Shower Baths, Douches of all sorts and the celebrated Mineral Water Aix Massage Bath and will afford, in addition to ordinary popular bathing facilities, every approved modern treatment of disorders of the Stomach, Liver and Kidneys, Gout, Rheumatism, Debility, Nervous Exhaustion, Hysteria, Anaemia, Scrofula, and other Cachexiae, including massage and electricity.*" By 1935 the treatments were no longer appearing to provide the miraculous cures of old and people drifted away in such numbers that the venture eventually closed down. Today the premises are the Kingswood Hotel.

A guide book from that golden era featured an advertisement for a firm who also made a healthy living from well-to-do people concerned about their appearance: "Established 1883. Gilbert E. Orman. Hair Dresser, Perfumer and Tobacconist, The Sidmouth Toilet Club, 1 Market Place, Sidmouth. Speciality in Hair Dressing for Balls, Soirees and Marriages, Wigs and Ornamental Hair Manufacture…" I guess running a business like that must have been a hair-raising experience at times!

Following the visit of the Russian princess, the famous Barrett family moved in, with eleven children and a reputedly tyrannical father, to 8 Fortfield Terrace and were to stay in residence for three years. Elizabeth Barrett-Browning soon fell in love with the resort and rode donkeys on the beach and even rowed all the way to Dawlish on one occasion. In particular she liked "the very land of green lanes and pretty thatched cottages with verandas and shrubberies, with sounds of the harp or piano coming through the windows." The Barrett family eventually returned to London and Elizabeth expressed her feelings for Sidmouth when she wrote: "Poor Sidmouth is left afar, I am almost inclined to say 'Poor Sidmouth'. Half my soul, in the meantime, seems to have stayed behind on the seashore, which I love more than ever now that I cannot walk upon it in the body."

There were rich men in Sidmouth, people like Mr Thomas L. Fish, a Victorian bachelor of substantial means. He lived at Knowle Cottage and surrounded himself with great treasures, the sort that would catch the eye of those experts you find on the *Antiques Roadshow*. In his garden he set up a small zoo which had kangaroos, cassowaries, marmosets and other creatures from all over the world. He opened his menagerie to the public on Monday afternoons from July to October.

He was quite content with his lot and did not see it necessary to venture far from his palatial home. However he was a great public benefactor and the local tradespeople were always indebted to him for the way that he looked after them. Therefore when he was burgled, they were not only surprised but shocked that someone who had done so much good had been wronged. It could well be this fact that nobody was prepared to accept the great and valuable collection of silverware that had been stolen from him. In

November 1853 a large sackful of silver was taken out of the River Sid and soon afterwards the rest was found a short way downstream.

With so many 'Gentlemen' residing in Sidmouth, it is not surprising that the very English game of cricket should have its place in the annals of local history. The town's cricket pavilion is one of the few thatched ones in the country and has entertained some interesting characters, not all of them famous for their prowess at cricket. Sir Arthur Conan-Doyle was a great enthusiast and turned out in guest appearances for the MCC when they sent representative teams all over England's green and pleasant wickets. Observant observers keeping a close eye on the score would once have seen it posted on a strange type of building, not exactly custom-made for the job as it was the last of a long line of bathing machines made redundant by the changing social scene and a mellowing of attitudes to public morality. Other visiting teams in those halcyon days included Crystal Palace, Will o' the Wisps, Devon Dumplings, The Nondescripts, Old Tonbridgians and The Ishmaelites.

The railways came late to Sidmouth and lasted less than a century. The opening ceremony on Monday, 6 July 1874 was colourful and the whole town bubbled with excitement. All the old codgers in the town were invited to a slap up lunch and tea at Knowle Grounds. To make their day a memorable occasion they were given a ride on the railway which cut through Harpford Woods before following the Otter Valley up to Sidmouth Junction (Feniton). A specially commemorated coin from the Royal Mint was doled out to all the senior citizens.

The procession to meet the first train to arrive, at 1.45 p.m. included marching bands and a thousand local schoolchildren.

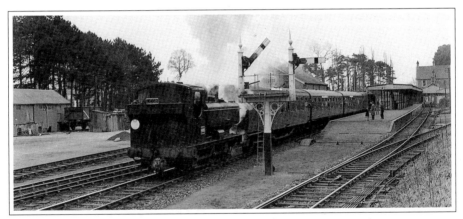

The link to the main line meant that journeys to London were now much easier and the improved communications resulted in a healthy boost for the resort.

The Duke of Connaught had the good sense to choose Sidmouth as his winter retreat in 1931 in preference to wintering on the French Riviera, where he owned a villa at Cap Ferrat. The stay was obviously a successful one as this royal octogenarian repeated it each year up to and including a stay in 1935. To have such an important person in the resort meant a lot to the local press who featured almost his every movement, from saying hello to mothers and babies on the sea front to attending events around the town with his Equerry, Major Berkeley Levett. By attending a rugby match, played between Sidmouth and Devonport Services 'A' team, he became the first Royal to attend such

a match in South West England! According to a report written long ago about the facilities at the Blackmore Field, the grandstand may have been comfortable but "the goal posts are good and excite the envy of visiting teams!"

His first winter was spent at the Fortfield Hotel but on later visits he stayed at the Manor House, which later became council offices.

A duty he was happy to perform was the opening of the Connaught Gardens as he had followed, with great interest, their adaptation from simply being the private grounds of 'Sea View' to becoming a public amenity appreciated by thousands of folk down through the years. On a fine, sunny morning all the various recesses of the Connaught Gardens are filled with people who sit and relax or admire the floral splendour of these gardens. The average age of its patrons is considerably higher than that of those who splash about in the sea at Jacob's Ladder Beach below.

The house which stood on the site before had a somewhat sinister reputation for it is believed that one of its former mistresses, Mrs Kent, was prone to bursts of insanity and was kept for long periods in a locked room. The rumours which spread around Sidmouth were of sufficient strength to prompt the family to leave the resort. A few years later the lady died in somewhat dubious circumstances... Even people unfamiliar with the house's reputation found it an unpleasant place to walk past and children dubbed it an 'Ogre's Castle'!

Beneath the house were lime kilns and at one time teams of donkeys worked from the shore unloading lime from Tor Bay to climb ramps to the kilns. The castellated tower is an imaginative adaptation built on top of the old lime kilns. From here the steps down to the beach became ruinous so it was decided to replace them with what locals soon started calling 'Jacob's Ladder'. This was a steep affair and those with a nervous disposition had a terrible time trying to go up or down. A less demanding structure was required and thus the second Jacob's Ladder provided an easier way of descending to the beach. However in 1939 the fear of a German invasion along the South Coast prompted all sorts of actions to thwart any possible invasion forces and Jacob's Ladder was removed. Following the war the present Ladder was constructed. If you ever try to identify when old views of Sidmouth from Peak Hill were photographed, all you have to do is to see which of the three 'Jacob's Ladders' are in place! These days most people gain access down to Jacob's Ladder Beach by the zig-zagging chine (a path cut in a cliff) that was created in the 1950s.

It is not only the rich and the aristocratic who have chosen to live in Sidmouth. R. F. Delderfield enjoyed great success with his West Country-based novels, three of them being adapted and serialised for television. *A Horseman Riding By*, *To Serve Them All My Days* and *Diana* used local settings and locations for filming. (Again, more details about these programmes made in the county can be found in *Made in Devon.*) Ronnie Delderfield had a cottage built for himself in 1967 on the upper slopes of Peak Hill, with tremendous eastward views along Lyme Bay. He called it 'The Gazebo', which means a look-out, and must have been such an ideal and inspiring retreat to pen such atmospheric stories.

Perhaps, then, you might imagine Sidmouth as being a rigidly, staunch Conservative stronghold but a glimmer of enlightenment shone through when Raving Loony Green Giant Party candidate, Stuart Hughes, was elected to the local council. To say he is a colourful character is a gross understatement, this political giant having triumphed against all the odds. His guest house is called, with a certain degree of intent to reflect its image, 'Fawlty Towers'. A Gloucestershire newly-wed couple, who availed themselves of the use of the four-poster bed, settled their bill simply by paying with four dozen eggs! The notion being, according to Loony Party logic, that any bride celebrating her pre-wedding with a 'hen' party should be permitted to pay for her post-wedding frolics with eggs! This little guest house in Temple Street, painted in the patriotic colours and style of the Union Flag, has witnessed many spectacles. At Christmas time a computerised snowstorm added to the festive spirit of the town, an attraction that brought coachloads of curious spectators to the town. When President Bush was in office it was learnt that the American president was a great *Fawlty Towers* fan so an invite to come and stay in the Sidmouth version was sent to him. Above all the charity work of Stuart Hughes should be appreciated and, although he may well be quite a 'Loony', he has, at least, done a lot of good work in this otherwise quiet, reserved and sedate resort. New businesses opening up in the town, are in the habit of employing his services for an opening ceremony with a difference.

Farther up the same street there were, in the late 1950s, two fish and chip shops, one run by an English family and the other by an Italian. A well known (in another part of Devon) newspaper proprietor grew up near these take-aways and would, as a mischievous teenager, enter the English cafe to buy his chips and then go into Luigi's to apply the Italian's salt and vinegar to them! It was fortunate for the lad that his turn of speed was greater than the Italian who always went through the motions of giving chase as far, at least, as the door to the premises.

Further proof that Sidmouth can stir itself from its slumbers has been evident in recent years when the town has attempted to log itself in the record books by trying to establish a world record for conga dancing. The fun began in 1977 when regatta week organisers invited the masses to assemble in a bid to beat the existing record, which was then held by Oklahoma University. Around 5,662 good conga folk joined together and the record was achieved in style. But records are as temporary as the shingle on Sidmouth's beach and others developed conga fever. The former Butlin's Holiday Camp at Filey, in Yorkshire, took away the record so Sidmouth and its conga army were conscripted into action again. The 8,128 writhing participants of 1978 enjoyed notching their place in the history books. The last conga we shall record in this little book is the amazing efforts of the 1984 snaking procession which employed another record breaking crowd of 9,286, one which extended the entire length of The Esplanade.

Strangely Sidmouth is not noted for possessing any number of ghosts, and its mysteries only verge on the minor scale of occurrences. The local police force were bamboozled, in 1990, by the disappearance of about four dozen yellow 'no waiting' cones. They had applied their keen, investigative wits but any amount of headscratching

Two aerial views – The top photo peers in from over the sea and looks straight up the Sid Valley. The bottom photo looks seaward and the River Sid can be seen running up the left side of the picture.

and logical thinking got them nowhere. Mr Viv Prince, a resident of Sidmouth who was, at various times, a drummer with The Kinks, The Pretty Things and The Who, couldn't understand why his garden was filled with the same yellow police cones! Then he saw his 'Lady', an Alsatian, deposit another and the riddle was solved! Someone with an eye for a newsworthy story for local television alerted the media who duly turned up to record it for TV consumption across the region. Unfortunately the film crew arrived about five minutes after a lorry had collected back the 'stolen' cones! A mystery which was not solved so easily was why 'Lady' only selected the police cones when there was ample opportunities to 'lift' some of the many red and white council cones in the town.

'Ram raiding' is a particularly destructive method of committing a robbery – the villain's vehicle being deliberately rammed through the windows of the targeted premises. The Consumer Market staff in Sidmouth must have thought they had been attacked in broad daylight in June 1992 when a Rover embedded itself in their shop. However the 74-year-old responsible did so by mistake. It is one of the perils of driving with the 'Krooklock' still on! Fortunately the runaway vehicle stopped a few feet short of hitting the startled shop assistants.

When Sidmouth sought a twin town there was a typical Euro-rumpus over British lamb and attempts to set up a twinning with a French town, at that time, proved difficult for Sidmouth. The solution of making links with a Swiss town meant that Sidmouth became only the second town in Britain to do so! Le Locle was twinned with Sidmouth in 1984. The Swiss town has a similar sized population but is not located on the Swiss coastline! The town's biggest employer is 'Tissot' who are a famous watchmaking firm.

In the summer months Sidmouth's repertory company puts on a range of entertainments at the Manor Theatre. For many seasons the Mercury Players held centre stage to captivate audiences with their thrillers and farces. However there have been others who have enjoyed the limelight here. Christabel Pankhurst, daughter of Emmeline, political leader of the suffragette movement, made an impassioned speech in this theatre on 22 March 1927. BBC Radio's *Any Questions* was broadcast from here in 1954. If only its walls could talk!

The town has had various places where films were shown but the Radway is the sole survivor and that only after a few hiccoughs along the way. The Grand Cinema in High Street, opened in 1929, was never quite as grand as its name suggested and, along with cinemas the length and breadth of the country, has long since closed down.

The Sidmouth Festival is billed as Europe's biggest international folk arts festival. Singers, dancers, musicians, entertainers and media personnel travel from all over the world to be involved in this superb event which brings Sidmouth to life. Staging it is a major organisational exercise but experience, which has been gradually accumulated since the first one in 1954, stands it in good stead. It provides a much needed boost to the local economy with the town packed to the door jambs with clog dancers, stilt dancers, Morris men, and performers of all shapes and sizes from all over the world. The pubs and the public gardens, the beach and the Esplanade ring to the sounds and sights of 'Folkies' having a wonderful time!

The River Sid, at about five miles long, is one of the shortest of Devon's many rivers and gives its name to several settlements like Sidbury, Sidford and Sidmouth. It rises, high in the hills, to the north of the town at a point in Pin Hill Woods about a half mile to the west of the Hare and Hounds pub on Gittisham Common. Here, in August 1951, a stone was rediscovered by a team of archaeologists. The stone is the subject of a local legend. It is believed that when the clock strikes twelve at midnight on Christmas Eve, the stone is supposed to roll down the hill to the head-waters of the River Sid (the sea in some versions) and then roll back again! The suggested reason for this journey is that witches are believed to have carried out sacrifices on this stone and, appalled by the event, it goes to cleanse itself of the blood which has been shed on it.

In its first mile the Sid drops sharply down through wooded country and it is in this area that, when heavy rainfall is recorded, the stream gathers great momentum and volume.

Sidbury is a lovely village of attractive 'sought-after' cottages set in a deep sheltered valley. In the past it was a more important community in relation to the district. It held a charter, believed to be the second oldest for a fair to be held, in the kingdom. A vestige of that former importance is the annual custom of hoisting a glove on a pole to signify the beginning of the two day event. The fair has historic roots which go back some five centuries. Attached to the event was the privilege for folk to more or less behave as they like, under the 'Hand of Freedom', for the duration of the fair, without the risk of being prosecuted for their misdemeanours!

The glove, which is older than most of the residents, is a big white one, which in the past was stuffed with sawdust, garlanded with flowers and had ribbons attached to it. In recent years it has been exhibited out of a top window of the Royal Oak. The main beneficiaries from the present celebrations are the children of the village school. All year long customers of the Royal Oak and the Red Lion donate small change so that when the glove is lifted, the old custom of throwing out hot pennies can take place. Armed with little pots and other receptacles, the children are divided into two age groups so as to ensure fair play. The main street is closed to traffic for the distribution of the coins and it is a well organised and civilised bit of traditional fun. There are two titles up for grabs– the junior champ and the senior champ– winners who often amass a tidy little sum of money.

The following day there is a sale of sheep, calves and pigs in the area beside the church wall. In the past other celebrations have included dances and skittle tournaments.

The church's spire possesses a weathercock that, on and off, has enjoyed one of the best views in the Sid Valley since 1728. In 1925, children making their way to school along the church path stumbled over the weathercock's tail. A storm the previous night, had broken it in two and had sent it crashing down from the top of the one hundred foot high spire. Luckily it had missed hitting anybody and the only damage had been to the tail itself. Local builder, Jim Brown, took it back to his workshop with every intention of putting it back as soon as the opportunity arose. Thirty or so years later Jim died and the weathercock was still at his works. When retiling work on the spire was carried out, in 1957, Mr Vanstone saw the chance to repair and relocate the weathercock atop the church once more. He removed the existing front end after a great deal of effort. In the thirty-two years that had elapsed since its tail had been blown off, it had been a useless indicator to the direction of the wind as it had stayed in a fixed position. The front end and back end were thus reunited and the heavy copper weathervane once more served

Sidbury. Mr Vanstone had done his bit for the 'retail' trade of the village!

An inscription in the church caused problems in respect that no learned person could work out the year of death of the person concerned. Try your luck with this. "To the memory of Henry Parson who died in the second-first climateric year of his age."

Griffith Ameridith was a man who owned property in the Sidbury area. He became Mayor of Exeter and, whilst carrying out his civic duties, came into contact with men who had been condemned to death for crimes that would barely have earned offenders probation these days. He was appalled at the way, even in death, the men were treated and wrote in his will that his Sidbury property should be sold off after his death and the monies raised should provide coffins for the executed men, thereby giving them a little dignity at their burials.

The present village hall was built in 1924 to replace Sidbury Iron Hall, which stood on the same site and became only fit for demolition. The lord of the manor, Sir Charles Henry Cave, provided the £3000 for this meeting place of quality with its many facilities, one that has been kept in an excellent state of repair. It has staged some unusual events, including in 1993, being the venue that 'kicked off' the 25th anniversary nationwide tour of the rock group called 'The Strawbs'. Probably their best known song is a tongue-in-cheek hit called *Part of the Union,* which will be with them 'till the day they die.' The real reason for such a big act to perform in such a small venue is that the group's lead singer, Dave Cousins, is a local man. One of his songs, *Glimpse of Heaven,* is about the beauty of this part of Devon, in particular Branscombe.

High on the hill above Sidbury is an Iron-age fort known, not surprisingly, as Sidbury Castle. It is a pear-shaped eminence measuring some 1,406 feet long and 430 feet wide. According to reference books it has two 'aggers' (ramparts) with a 'fosse' between them. It is the largest of many hill forts in the district and it gives its name to the village!

In 1815, when everyone was worried about a possible French invasion, every time a French ship was spied off Sidmouth the ladies of the village donned red cloaks, grabbed their brooms and massed on Castle Hill. The logic for this unusual act was that, seen from a distance, these ladies looked like a regiment of troops armed ready for combat. This would appear to have done the trick!

Sidford is the village where Sidbury FC play. It sits astride the main Exeter to Lyme Regis road (A3052) and is now a suburb of a greater Sidmouth, which has spread right up the Sid Valley. In days of old, when it was a smaller satellite of Sidbury, it was a den of inequity with smuggled goods stowed away from the prying eyes of the coastguard. Indeed a pit measuring 8 x 6 feet could and did accommodate a great number of barrels of brandy. The pit was so well covered over that on one occasion coastguards, who were wont to poke their detecting rods anywhere in the hope or expectation of finding a cache of goods, poked this spot – and never realised how close they came to the jackpot!

King Charles II is believed to have spent a night in the village following the Battle of Worcester. In his hurry to get on, he left one of his gloves behind. The ardent Royalist mistress of the cottage, near the Sid, left it in the room and every time she entered she would do a curtsy to it! Another story attached to this alleged visit is that the King's horse lost a shoe so he reported to the local blacksmith. He noticed that the horse's

shoes were all the wrong way round. On being quizzed, the King told him that this was a deliberate ploy to send anyone following him the wrong way!

Despite the village's dubious reputation there was no policeman, the burden of surveillance duties falling on the shoulders of a cobbler who doubled up as a special constable. In his spare time he spied on his fellow villagers. He was suspicious of someone called Godfrey and, as things turned out, caught him red-handed delivering contraband. For reporting the smuggler he received £30. Godfrey was punished but had not learnt his lesson so was again caught by the cobbler (singular!). The events followed a similar course but by now the Sidford folk were fed up with the informant and vowed revenge. Between them they made it look as if the cobbler and his wife had mistreated their children, a plausible ploy, which earned the couple six months in Exeter Gaol. They came out and started life afresh at Windwhistle and their immense unpopularity

lead to the locals there doing exactly the same again. It's not often that a cobbler gets stitched up himself!

Sidford's present bridge has carried traffic since 1930. The original pack-horse bridge has been incorporated into the present bridge's structure. The previous bridge was hump-backed and, when taken too quickly by those coming speedily down Trow Hill, was a dangerous proposition.

The Sid now has the added flows of tributaries like the Roncombe Stream and the Snod Brook and has been known to cause great mischief, particularly lower down in the more populated parts of its valley. Locals have perpetuated a fable that the Roncombe stream has human characteristics and that, because murders and other dark and dastardly deeds have been committed in the deep sinister hollow where the watercourse rises, it has a mind to do no good. Many a time it has tried to undo any of man's efforts to control it in its lower reaches. 'Lord Roncombe' vents his anger by washing away bridges, causing floods and being a general nuisance.

Floods have always been a problem and older Sid Valley dwellers will recall 1960 when many places in East Devon were thrown into chaos as all the rivers, the Sid included, went on the rampage. Although a flood alleviation scheme has been in place for some years now, it did not help to prevent the removal of handrails to 'Heart's Delight Bridge' in 1989. A tree carried by the spate removed them with greater adeptness than the most practised of vandals. However the bridge, which was built in 1936 to allow residents from the built-up side of the Sid access to the beautiful meadows known as The Byes (their Heart's Delight!), is now restored to even better condition than it was before. One in the eye for 'Lord Roncombe' – for the time being…

In Sidmouth's Eastern Town many houses have slots by their front doors so that if and when there is a flood alert, they can insert boards to help keep out the flood waters. Sand bags placed in front afford even greater protection for residents who live closest to the river. When the river is in torrent it is a foolish person that uses the famous ford at Mill Street. Even worse is to break down in the  middle, like this poor chap who could really have used the AA (Amphibious Association) or the RAC (River Automobile Club) to help him out of his watery predicament!

A short distance away is the lowest bridging point over the Sid, in the shape of the three-arched pedestrian Alma Bridge. The Crimean War Battle of Alma took place on Wednesday, 20 September 1854 with men from the Devonshire Regiment amongst the two thousand who perished in the first two hours of combat. The bridge was duly named to commemorate this conflict when built a year later. The *Laurel* had gone aground on Sidmouth's beach and, whilst resting on its laurels, started to be broken up by the sea. So rather than waste a good wreck, its timbers were shaped into the first Alma Bridge. By the turn of the century it had deteriorated into a sad state of repair so the present bridge replaced it. It affords pedestrian access for those who wish to carry on their coastal perambulation and is the official point where the sea begins; fall off the north side and you land in the river, fall of a few feet away on the south side and you are in the old briny! This is all academic to the ducks, waterfowl or swans that swim to and fro beneath the bridge.

Years ago the River Sid did not discharge into the sea at this point, opting to issue a few hundred yards or so farther west. The river has changed its course and its function – no longer does it have a great number of mills like it used to possess. The street names of Sidmouth that include 'mill' in them are evidence of these former establishments.

The lower Sid once was an estuary but, with a blocked mouth, soon silted up to create the land on which the oldest part of the resort stands.

Once a year the 'wild life' of the River Sid is given a major boost as thousands of ducks appear, float down the river and then disappear for another twelve months. The occurrence is the brainchild of the local Lions Club who have raised many thousands

of pounds for local charities since 1985. The idea is for people to sponsor a yellow plastic duck as it sails down the Sid, hoping to win a short race between Sid Park Bridge and Waterloo Bridge. The event takes place on the last Sunday afternoon in July and what began with a thousand ducks has soared to five thousand. This is now the upper limit, thus assuring keen competition to 'own' one. The only non yellow one permitted is a red one sponsored by local TV and radio personality, Ian Brass. In 1992 one poor little yellow duck dodged the spectators and officials. It even managed to get out of the congested mouth of the River Sid to remain at large for nine months. After a winter of bobbing about in Lyme Bay, it was washed up onto the beach, just a few miles away at Littlecombe Shoot, Branscombe – clearly it was a homing duck!

The ducks are locally owned and 'live' in the Sid Valley. From time to time they are hired out for other events and have made guest appearances at Manchester and in South Devon where they 'performed' for a Telethon event.

In the past travelling circuses have been staged in The Byes. At such times slightly larger creatures than ducks have been witnessed in the River Sid as elephants had their daily bath. So as not to offend the local population, they always kept their trunks on!

One of the best walks in the district is over Mutter's Moor, a high common above the western side of the town. Abraham Mutter was an associate of the legendary smuggler, Jack Rattenbury (see *Around and About Seaton and Beer*). He cut turf and felled timber on what is now Mutter's Moor. He was an industrious man who hawked his products all over East Devon; with his carts and his donkeys he was a familiar sight in Exeter, Exmouth and Sidmouth. Rattenbury was always on the look-out to improve the distribution service for his illicitly imported cargoes, notably of brandy. What better cloak of secrecy could there possibly be than a cloak of turf! Rattenbury persuaded Mutter to be one of his carriers. He did rather well out of the extra trade and when Rattenbury retired, to Sidmouth, Abraham, assisted by other members of the family, carried on the trade.

The coast road from Sidmouth over Peak Hill to Otterton has been subjected to erosion throughout the years and its line has been altered to stay out of the clutches of a relentless sea, which gnaws away at the cliff-line all the time. The sea off Sidmouth is often stained a deep red colour, the product of sandstone worn from the cliffs. Peak Hill is long and steep, even steeper if you have to walk up it! The car park at the top with its flinty "I'm going to get your tyres" surface is a popular one with those who like to go for a stroll on Mutter's Moor and across Bulverton Hill. There is hardly a walking book published about East Devon, that doesn't feature this well used route, this little conveyor belt of dog-walking terrestrials. *Ten Family Walks in East Devon* however, has managed to leave it out in the hope that locals will try pastures new (it is an absolute 'must' for anyone who enjoys a stroll of just a few hours!)

Just beyond the car park is probably the best westward-looking view in Devon. Those who are familiar with the Devonshire landscape will be able, on a clear day, to spy Berry Head just beyond Brixham, the range of the Haldon Hills to the west of the Exe Estuary and, beyond them, distinctive Dartmoor peaks like Haytor Rocks, Rippon Tor, Hameldown Ridge (high above Widecombe in the Moor) and Cawsand Beacon (Cosdon) at the northern end of Dartmoor – what a view! Locals slow up noticeably as they start the long drop down towards Otterton. Those who stroll the coastal footpath, or who plod along to Mutter's Moor and beyond, can savour even more expansive views at their leisure.

The road twists and turns to Otterton. It was never designed to carry the present flow of traffic that uses it. Consequently there are now numerous passing places gouged out of the hedgerows to permit people, in their private chariots, an easier passage through to Otterton.

Otterton is well worth reaching! It is one of the most attractive villages in the county, a place where many visitors like to walk up the main street, the Otterton Brook trickling beside it, to look at the 'chocolate-box', 'picture-postcard' cottages, each one different to its neighbour.

This idyllic scene was transformed in July 1968 when a prolonged downpour swelled the little stream so quickly that its banks could not contain it. The flow inundated the entire width of the broad main thoroughfare then, when the floods subsided, a volume of silt, earth and rubble was left behind. It took many hours of cleaning up to restore the village back to its pristine condition.

The stream was fortunately not in spate when, one morning in January 1990, a bus was found in it! It is believed that the handbrake had not been properly applied and it just trundled into the Otterton Brook of its own volition. Nobody was hurt.

One of the saddest stories to come out of Otterton happened a long time ago but this does not diminish a local tragedy. The young man was so happy to make the girl of his dreams his wife as they strolled out of Otterton's hillside church, arm in arm, ready to start on life's great adventure together. They lived at a time when the roads were just mud tracks, when money was in even shorter supply than it is now and when a honeymoon was out of the question for a poor farm lad and his 'maid'. But they were determined to make the most out of the occasion and arranged to take a boat from

Ladram Bay to Sidmouth. Several of their friends accompanied them and a great time was had by all at an inn in Sidmouth. Evening came and the merry little ensemble started back home. Unfortunately a sudden squall blew up and one of the young men lost his hat overboard. In a bid to regain it, he inadvertently capsized the small boat and everyone was thrown into the sea. Seven of the revellers were drowned, including the bride. The bridegroom survived the ordeal by managing to swim ashore, but he remained emotionally scarred for the rest of his life.

The demon drink led to another tragedy in this quiet Devon village. Whether or not

the story is true is not known but a man who was drunk returned home and, in a fit of pique, murdered his wife. He then fled to Sidmouth where he carried on his drunken binge in a hostelry. By the time he had finished he didn't know what day of the week it was and could not remember the awful crime that he had committed.

The law, though, was less forgetful and at Ottery St Mary he was found guilty and condemned to death, the 'execution' place being his native Otterton so that justice could be seen to be done. The sentence differed from the normal straightforward hanging as, instead of having a noose placed around his neck, he was placed in a cage, which was dangled from a gibbet, and starved to death! A minding fee was paid to those who vigilantly ensured that no food was smuggled to him!

However it is not death and disaster that has resulted in Otterton having a lower population today than it did in the mid nineteenth century. Then it had eight shops, three bakers, a coal merchant and many blacksmiths. It was also a thriving agricultural community with a hundred acres of cider orchards providing work for many people, large numbers of hogsheads of cider being produced to send Devonians, and other more distant consumers into that delightful state of oblivion induced by this heady substance. Indeed it was rumoured that cattle bingeing on cider apples gobbled up in an orchard occasionally got tipsy, but it is more likely that it was the occasional intake of the resultant 'apple cheese' from the manufacturing process of cider making that caused red faced black-faced sheep!

A cattle market used to be held on The Green where animals were tethered to the chestnut trees prior to being sold for the Christmas market.

The women of the village were busily engaged in lace making and their nimble fingerwork brought orders from far afield. The village declined in size but today is seen as a lovely place to retire to and there are a great number of folk who speak without the strong Devon accent that was so prevalent when Otterton was an almost self-contained and self-sufficient country village, half a day's travel, on foot, away from the metropolis of Exeter.

Visitors like to stroll around and with a copy of *Ten Family Walks in East Devon*, you can follow a longer walk in and around Otterton. It has a bit of village, a few lanes, the odd hill (best glossed over!), some coastline and a riverside stretch. End of commercial!

Otterton Mill, beside the River Otter, is an attraction worth visiting. To open it as a working tourist attraction was the idea of Mrs Desna Greenhow and the well known Judge Polson. Alas the judge died, but the mill has been successful and apart from milling, which goes on regularly, it houses other arts and skills of talented people in the mill's studio workshops. The Mill Museum is an educational and entertaining experience; the Miller tells a good tale!

Otterton is very conscious of its appearance and, along with many other Devon villages, enters 'The Best Kept Village' competition. In 1991 it came first in the category of 'villages with a population of more than 500', beating fifty-eight other would-be contenders for the prestigious title.

Ladram Bay is a popular spot, many of the visitors to its caravan park coming back year after year. Large sea stacks jut out boldly from the water, the habitat of many sea birds. The principal piles are called Picket Rock, Little Picket and Man of God Rock. The sea continually buffets them so in time they will collapse and be removed from the scene.

There have been various spellings for Ladram with Larderham and Ladderham being just two of them. The latter is believed to have derived from the fact that this was yet another haven of smuggling and that 'ladders' were used to convey the goods up the cliff. It could well be that the aptly-named Brandy Head, a short distance from Ladram, is another place name clue to the nefarious goings-on in days long gone! The last known smuggler here was Amos Gibbs of Muttersmire Farm (now corrupted to Muttersmoor). His father was also one and lost his life trying to land cargo at Ladram in a storm. The risk was taken because it was thought that the Revenue cutter would probably not leave port, Exmouth or Sidmouth, in such atrocious conditions. After a few scares, Amos packed in his own smuggling career and achieved old age.

Up to 1830 an annual Fair was held at Ladram on the Wednesday after Easter. The seaside celebrations included revels of all descriptions, a favourite attraction being wrestling matches, with locals trying their luck against the professionals of the day.

In 1987 a local beachcomber struck gold at Sandy Cove, a short distance east of Ladram's beach. His find was the first Viking discovery in this area and the ring, found below the high water mark, was deemed his property and realised £3,000 for him!

Salcombe Regis is usually referred to as Salcombe, but should not be confused with its namesake, a yachtsmen's paradise in the most southern part of Devon. *This* Salcombe is about a mile from Sidmouth, the other side of Salcombe Hill Cliff. In its graveyard are some interesting and unusual characters...

John Yonge Anderson-Morhead (1846-1923) in his *History of Salcombe Regis* included some bizarre observations about the church graveyard where, apparently, five typhus victims were buried. Nearby lies the corpse of the gypsy who brought the virus to the village. His body was pegged to the ground with two iron bars, presumably to prevent him going on a ghostly walkabout to spread the epidemic further!

The grave of James Page is a reminder that high cliffs and a scant respect for the laws of gravity form a lethal partnership. His short life was brought to an abrupt halt in May 1828 when he tried to secrete some game fowl eggs in a jackdaw's nest. Unfortunately the jackdaw had chosen a cliff-top aerie and poor James overshot it and plummeted from Maynard's Cliff onto the beach below.

Anderson-Morhead's own words tell us that even Victorian holidaymakers like to take home the 'odd' souvenir of their visit... "*The Hooper's Vault skeletons are only 18 inches underground, but the men are all over six feet tall. There were eleven skulls until a Tourist took one, so now there are ten.*"

Local lady, Miriam Bannister, was baptised at Salcombe Regis church in 1817 and managed to live until 1928, a span of 111 years and 'no passes'! Also buried here is Sir Norman Lockyer whose Observatory, on Salcombe Hill, is a splendid institution and well worth a visit. And talking of seeing things...

The mind can play tricks on you if you are out in the open in fog; things you would never look at twice in the landscape, take on a new dimension and an altogether different appearance. Salcombe Regis's Parish Clerk made a journey in the district in such conditions and was stopped dead in his tracks atop the mist-enveloped Soldiers Hill. The horrible sight that confronted him was the Devil! The clerk loudly cried out, "Halt Satan!" and proceeded to do the equivalent of an evangelical sales pitch highlighting his own strongly held religious convictions. He proclaimed, with great fervour, his devotion to Him above. Then it slowly dawned on him that this was not the Devil, nor foul fiend to daunt his spirit, but a plain ordinary donkey – he must have felt a bit of an ass! When the story got around, he was given the nickname 'Halt Satan' and it was only his vile threats to prosecute those who persisted to taunt him, that saw the jibe dropped!

Salcombe Regis has had a few ghosts. Two white ladies used to haunt the church path and a Mr Lydes caused quite a stir. Apparently he was greatly upset to hear a robin singing whilst he was prostrate on his death bed. He started cursing and swearing and in the process slipped loudly and blasphemously into death. The Good Lord was obviously none too keen to accept a spirit in such a foul mood, specially when the man's anger had been vented at one of His little creatures. At the funeral supper, Lydes' spirit reappeared. Attending were two Cambridge-educated priests who promptly tried to exorcise the spirit but to no avail. Another priest was summoned. Oxford-educated, George Cornish banished Lydes's ghost for at least sixty years, a suitable cooling off period.

There are numerous examples of ghosts in Devon leading people to treasure. Salcombe's benevolent ghost was a lady who was seen regularly, up to 1820, drifting around a field close to the junction of the Salcombe and Lyme roads. A farmer sighted her as he was ploughing his field with a team of oxen when, to his horror, one disappeared before his very eyes. The poor creature had fallen down a hole, and extricating it required a great deal of effort. But it was all worthwhile as, when the farmer peered into the chasm, he could not believe his eyes – stashed there was a fortune in booty! His family enjoyed the fruits of his windfall or 'ox' fall and the lady ghost was never seen again!

Spirits have caused more than their share of upset in this parish. The village's main source of income at one time was the manufacture of cider – but there wasn't a pub!

The illegal importing of brandy eventually got them into all sorts of trouble. They had the perfect hiding place for their goods in the tower of the church! An added bonus was the parish clerk – 'Old Pike' whose brief it was to keep a vigilant look-out for any goings-on. His powers of surveillance were somewhat limited as the old boy was blind!

One dark night smugglers were busily occupied raising casks up the cliff when they felt a tug on the rope. Assuming it to be one of their own, they started pulling their colleague towards the cliff top. When he came into sight they realised he was a coastguard and in their panic they let go and sent the poor man down over the 500 feet high cliffs to his death. After that they lost heart in their trade and, aware of even greater surveillance of their activities, stopped smuggling on a large scale.

The best rendition, which I have heard, about the smuggling antics in this district came from the verger of Salcombe Regis Church, Michael Thomson. He has committed a transcript to heart, and uses it to entertain visitors in the summer. His daughter is Mary Thomson, Olympic Games and international showjumper.

The most imposing landmarks in Exeter have a strong connection with Salcombe Regis. The mediaeval twin towers of Exeter Cathedral are made out of stone from the virtually disused Dunscombe Quarry in this parish. Pete Dare, chief stonemason at the Cathedral, wanted to carry out renovation work to the south tower in 1980 but to do so he felt that he would have to use the same stone so as not to spoil the appearance. After a year of detective work, he found Dunscombe and arranged to lift agreed amounts to carry out the repairs. The deal only permitted extracting the rock in the winter months as the quarry was a caravan park in the summer months! The quarry had also been re-opened in 1930 to take out stone to build the church of St Francis at nearby Woolbrook.

Salcombe Regis has been put on the map in recent decades by the stirling efforts of Mrs Elizabeth Svendson to improve the plight of mistreated donkeys, and also to provide riding for the disabled. The Donkey Sanctuary was opened in 1970 and became a registered charity some three years later. It has directly helped many thousands of donkeys and Mrs Svendson's globe-trotting mercy missions have won publicity, and a greater degree of protection world-wide for these four-legged friends.

There have been many guests to view the impressive facilities and these include Arthur Negus, who will always be remembered for his great knowledge and enthusiasm for antiques, which he communicated over the television for a number of years. He was a patron of the charity and visited the annual donkey fiesta in 1981. Four years later Princess Anne inspected the work of the centre. People love animals and no better proof is needed than the figures that revealed this charity, according to one survey, had received more bequests than Oxfam!

We have now reached the end of our exploration 'around and about Sidmouth'. If you want to carry on the eastward continuation of this journey, then you should purchase the equivalent book that features Branscombe, Beer, Seaton and Colyton. This is called, not surprisingly, *Around and About Seaton and Beer.*

OTHER OBELISK PUBLICATIONS THAT FEATURE THIS AREA:

Ten Family Walks in East Devon, Sally & Chips Barber   32pp   £1.95

Around & About Seaton and Beer, Chips Barber   32pp   £2.50

Tales of the Unexplained in Devon, Judy Chard   48pp   £2.50

Made in Devon, Chips Barber and David FitzGerald   104pp   £2.99
